This Planning Guide Belongs to: _____

TC Publishing Inc.
PO Box 290686
Columbia, SC 29229

Printed in the United States of America
Published simultaneously in paperback and ebook by TC Publishing Inc.
First edition of this translation, 2021

Cover Photo Credit: Jen Roberson Photography

Paperback ISBN 978-0-578-90465-8
Ebook ISBN 978-0-578-90466-5

TOYIACAISE.COM

If you need to SNATCH back your peace, serenity, and sanity... this guide is for you! Taking care of yourself is so important, as many times, we nurturers hurry along meeting the needs of so many that we fail to look out for ourselves. Well, no worries boo, I got you! This guide will help:

- Plan out your day
- Give you a road map to success
- Provide self-care reminders
- Give you check lists to help keep you on track
- Prompt you for daily check-ins
- Provide journal pad prompts
- & More!

I used this guide to help me breathe again after the loss of my sister. I know just how overwhelming one day can be, so grab you a hot cup of coffee/tea, sit back, and meditate on all things Y O U!

Please note: Time is purposely removed from the planner, as it is designed for and around you!

The daily and monthly planners are located just before the Road Map to Success Sections.

Happy Planning

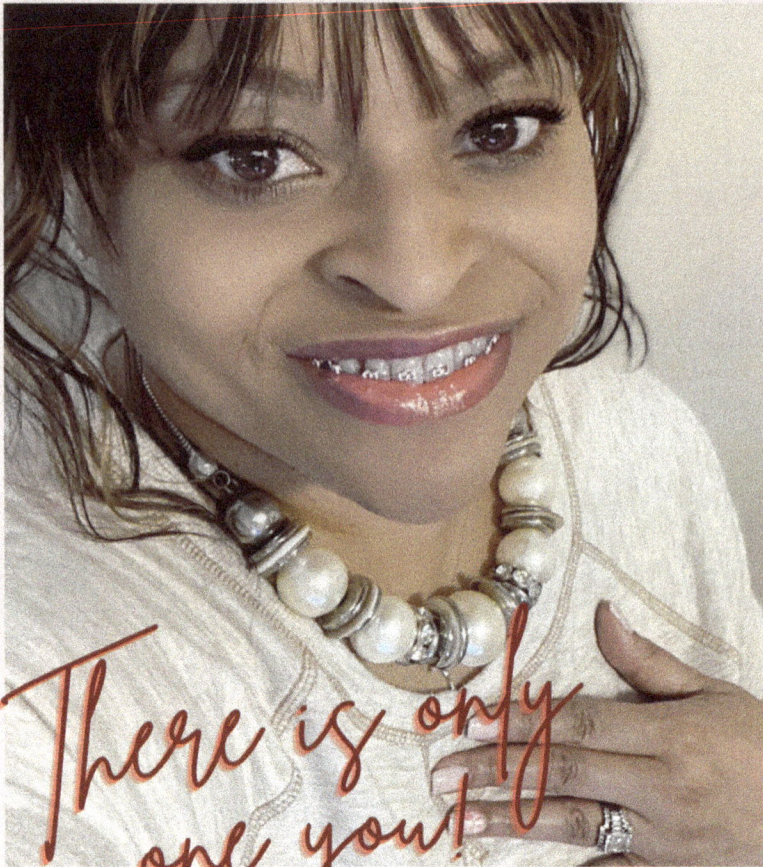

There is only one you!

Thank you for taking this time to care for yourself. I have been right where you are now. I had to learn to step back, consider my star-player, and take care of myself first. It was hard, but well worth it! I pray this guide will assist you along your journey to caring for yourself. Remember, there is only one you and when you are depleted, you are unable to help anyone. Take care of you!

Toyia

Self Care Routine

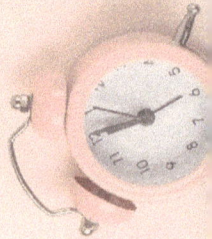

DO SOMETHING TODAY THAT YOUR FUTURE SELF WILL THANK YOU FOR.

Our actions and decisions today will shape the way we will be living in the future.

30 Days of Happiness

Fill Your Month with Self-Care

Each square represents one day of the month. Mark the box when you have fulfilled the day. Let's try to leave no box unchecked!

Take a walk	Practice breathing exercises	Read a good book or article	Try something new	Sleep in or go to bed early
Do something creative	Eat your favorite meal	Spend time in outdoors	Chat with an old friend	Write down 3 things you are grateful for
Pamper yourself	Declutter and donate	Watch your favorite movie	Stretch	Take a digital detox day
Cuddle up and read a good book	Listen to your favorite music	Take 5 minutes to breathe and be still	Say No	Say Yes
Plan Your Next Vacation	Do something fun	Random Act of Kindness	Listen to a Podcast	Create a list of short term goals
Drink Enough Water	Take a Nap	Watch a sunrise or sunset	Do something you loved as a child	Dress up; just because

DAILY PLANNER SECTION

Daily Planner

M	T	W	T	F	S	S

Reminder:

Today's Big Goal

Personal To Do List

○ ....
○ ....
○ ....
○ ....
○ ....
○ ....
○ ....

To Do List

○ ....
○ ....
○ ....
○ ....
○ ....
○ ....
○ ....
○ ....
○ ....
○ ....

Notes

Today's Mood

Very happy   Neutral   Not great

Productivity Level

0%   30%   70%   100%

Positivity Planner

Tasks for Today

- ☐ _____
- ☐ _____
- ☐ _____
- ☐ _____
- ☐ _____
- ☐ _____
- ☐ _____

Notes to Self

_____

_____

_____

_____

Daily Planner

M	T	W	T	F	S	S

Reminder:

Today's Big Goal

Personal To Do List

- ◯
- ◯
- ◯
- ◯
- ◯
- ◯
- ◯

To Do List

- ◯
- ◯
- ◯
- ◯
- ◯
- ◯
- ◯
- ◯
- ◯
- ◯

Notes

Today's Mood

Very happy   Neutral   Not great

Productivity Level

0%   30%   70%   100%

Positivity Planner

Tasks for Today

- ☐ _____
- ☐ _____
- ☐ _____
- ☐ _____
- ☐ _____
- ☐ _____
- ☐ _____

Notes to Self

_____

_____

_____

_____

_____

I'm grateful for...

Daily Planner

M	T	W	T	F	S	S

Reminder:

Today's Big Goal

Personal To Do List

- ○
- ○
- ○
- ○
- ○
- ○
- ○

To Do List

- ○
- ○
- ○
- ○
- ○
- ○
- ○
- ○
- ○
- ○

Notes

Today's Mood

Very happy   Neutral   Not great

Productivity Level

0%   30%   70%   100%

Positivity Planner

Tasks for Today

☐ _____

☐ _____

☐ _____

☐ _____

☐ _____

☐ _____

☐ _____

Notes to Self

_____

_____

_____

_____

Daily Planner

M	T	W	T	F	S	S

Reminder:

Today's Big Goal

Personal To Do List

- ○
- ○
- ○
- ○
- ○
- ○

To Do List

- ○
- ○
- ○
- ○
- ○
- ○
- ○
- ○
- ○
- ○
- ○

Notes

Today's Mood

Very happy   Neutral   Not great

Productivity Level

0%   30%   70%   100%

Positivity Planner

Tasks for Today

- [ ] _____
- [ ] _____
- [ ] _____
- [ ] _____
- [ ] _____
- [ ] _____
- [ ] _____

Notes to Self

_____

_____

_____

_____

Daily Planner

M	T	W	T	F	S	S

Reminder:

Today's Big Goal

Personal To Do List

- ○
- ○
- ○
- ○
- ○
- ○
- ○

To Do List

- ○
- ○
- ○
- ○
- ○
- ○
- ○
- ○
- ○
- ○

Notes

Today's Mood

Very happy   Neutral   Not great

Productivity Level

0%   30%   70%   100%

Positivity Planner

Tasks for Today

- [ ] _____
- [ ] _____
- [ ] _____
- [ ] _____
- [ ] _____
- [ ] _____
- [ ] _____

Notes to Self

_____

_____

_____

_____

Daily Planner

M	T	W	T	F	S	S

Reminder:

Today's Big Goal

Personal To Do List

- ○
- ○
- ○
- ○
- ○
- ○
- ○

To Do List

- ○
- ○
- ○
- ○
- ○
- ○
- ○
- ○
- ○
- ○

Notes

Today's Mood

Very happy   Neutral   Not great

Productivity Level

0%   30%   70%   100%

Positivity Planner

Tasks for Today

☐ _____

☐ _____

☐ _____

☐ _____

☐ _____

☐ _____

☐ _____

Notes to Self

_____

_____

_____

_____

_____

Daily Planner

Reminder:

Today's Big Goal

Personal To Do List

- ○ ....
- ○ ....
- ○ ....
- ○ ....
- ○ ....
- ○ ....
- ○ ....

To Do List

- ○ ....
- ○ ....
- ○ ....
- ○ ....
- ○ ....
- ○ ....
- ○ ....
- ○ ....
- ○ ....
- ○ ....
- ○ ....

Notes

Today's Mood

Very happy   Neutral   Not great

Productivity Level

0%   30%   70%   100%

TOYIACAISE.COM

Positivity Planner

Tasks for Today

- [ ] _____
- [ ] _____
- [ ] _____
- [ ] _____
- [ ] _____
- [ ] _____
- [ ] _____

Notes to Self

_____

_____

_____

_____

Daily Planner

M	T	W	T	F	S	S

Reminder:

Today's Big Goal

To Do List
- ◯
- ◯
- ◯
- ◯
- ◯
- ◯
- ◯
- ◯
- ◯
- ◯
- ◯

Personal To Do List
- ◯
- ◯
- ◯
- ◯
- ◯
- ◯

Notes

Today's Mood

Very happy   Neutral   Not great

Productivity Level

0%   30%   70%   100%

Positivity Planner

Tasks for Today

☐ _____

☐ _____

☐ _____

☐ _____

☐ _____

☐ _____

☐ _____

Notes to Self

_____

_____

_____

_____

Daily Planner

M	T	W	T	F	S	S

Reminder:

Today's Big Goal

To Do List
- ○
- ○
- ○
- ○
- ○
- ○
- ○
- ○
- ○
- ○

Personal To Do List
- ○
- ○
- ○
- ○
- ○
- ○

Notes

Today's Mood

Very happy　　　　　Neutral　　　　　Not great

Productivity Level

0%　　　　30%　　　　70%　　　　100%

Positivity Planner

Tasks for Today

☐ _____

☐ _____

☐ _____

☐ _____

☐ _____

☐ _____

☐ _____

Notes to Self

_____

_____

_____

_____

_____

Daily Planner

M	T	W	T	F	S	S

Reminder:

Today's Big Goal

Personal To Do List

- ◯
- ◯
- ◯
- ◯
- ◯
- ◯
- ◯

To Do List

- ◯
- ◯
- ◯
- ◯
- ◯
- ◯
- ◯
- ◯
- ◯
- ◯

Notes

Today's Mood

Very happy   Neutral   Not great

Productivity Level

0%   30%   70%   100%

Positivity Planner

Tasks for Today

☐ _____

☐ _____

☐ _____

☐ _____

☐ _____

☐ _____

☐ _____

Notes to Self

_____

_____

_____

_____

I'm grateful for...

Daily Planner

M	T	W	T	F	S	S

Reminder:

Today's Big Goal

Personal To Do List

- ◯ ....
- ◯ ....
- ◯ ....
- ◯ ....
- ◯ ....
- ◯ ....

To Do List

- ◯ ....
- ◯ ....
- ◯ ....
- ◯ ....
- ◯ ....
- ◯ ....
- ◯ ....
- ◯ ....
- ◯ ....
- ◯ ....
- ◯ ....

Notes

Today's Mood

😆 😋 🙂 😐 😒 😫

⟵——————————————⟶

Very happy   Neutral   Not great

Productivity Level

⚡ ⚡ ⚡ ⚡ ⚡ ⚡ ⚡ ⚡ ⚡ ⚡

⟵——————————————⟶

0%   30%   70%   100%

TOYIACAISE.COM

Positivity Planner

I'm grateful for...

Tasks for Today

- ☐ _____
- ☐ _____
- ☐ _____
- ☐ _____
- ☐ _____
- ☐ _____
- ☐ _____

Notes to Self

_____

_____

_____

_____

TOYIACAISE.COM

Daily Planner

M	T	W	T	F	S	S

Reminder:

Today's Big Goal

Personal To Do List

- ◯
- ◯
- ◯
- ◯
- ◯
- ◯
- ◯

To Do List

- ◯
- ◯
- ◯
- ◯
- ◯
- ◯
- ◯
- ◯
- ◯
- ◯

Notes

Today's Mood

Very happy   Neutral   Not great

Productivity Level

0%   30%   70%   100%

Positivity Planner

Tasks for Today

- [ ] _____
- [ ] _____
- [ ] _____
- [ ] _____
- [ ] _____
- [ ] _____
- [ ] _____

Notes to Self

_____

_____

_____

_____

Daily Planner

M	T	W	T	F	S	S

Reminder:

Today's Big Goal

Personal To Do List

- ◯
- ◯
- ◯
- ◯
- ◯
- ◯
- ◯

To Do List

- ◯
- ◯
- ◯
- ◯
- ◯
- ◯
- ◯
- ◯
- ◯
- ◯

Notes

Today's Mood

😆 😛 🙂 😐 😔 😫

Very happy   Neutral   Not great

Productivity Level

⚡ ⚡ ⚡ ⚡ ⚡ ⚡ ⚡ ⚡ ⚡ ⚡

0%   30%   70%   100%

Positivity Planner

Tasks for Today

- [ ] _____
- [ ] _____
- [ ] _____
- [ ] _____
- [ ] _____
- [ ] _____
- [ ] _____

Notes to Self

_____

_____

_____

_____

Daily Planner

M	T	W	T	F	S	S

Reminder:

Today's Big Goal

Personal To Do List

- ○
- ○
- ○
- ○
- ○
- ○
- ○

To Do List

- ○
- ○
- ○
- ○
- ○
- ○
- ○
- ○
- ○
- ○
- ○

Notes

Today's Mood

Very happy   Neutral   Not great

Productivity Level

0%   30%   70%   100%

Positivity Planner

Tasks for Today

- [ ] _____
- [ ] _____
- [ ] _____
- [ ] _____
- [ ] _____
- [ ] _____
- [ ] _____

Notes to Self

_____

_____

_____

_____

_____

Daily Planner

M | T | W | T | F | S | S

Reminder:

Today's Big Goal

Personal To Do List

- ○ ....
- ○ ....
- ○ ....
- ○ ....
- ○ ....
- ○ ....
- ○

To Do List

- ○ ....
- ○ ....
- ○ ....
- ○ ....
- ○ ....
- ○ ....
- ○ ....
- ○ ....
- ○ ....
- ○ ....
- ○

Notes

Today's Mood

Very happy   Neutral   Not great

Productivity Level

0%   30%   70%   100%

Positivity Planner

Tasks for Today

- [ ] _____
- [ ] _____
- [ ] _____
- [ ] _____
- [ ] _____
- [ ] _____
- [ ] _____

Notes to Self

_____

_____

_____

_____

just breathe

Sometimes, all we need to do is step back and just breathe before we speak or react. Practice makes perfect!

MONTHLY PLANNING SHEETS

Monthly Calendar

Month: _____

Year: _____

Goals:

Notes:

_____

_____

_____

_____

_____

_____

Monthly Calendar

Month: _____   Year: _____

Goals:

Notes:

_____

_____

_____

_____

_____

_____

Monthly Calendar

Month: _____   Year: _____

Goals:

Notes:

_____

_____

_____

_____

_____

Monthly Calendar

Month: _____   Year: _____

Goals:

Notes:

_____

_____

_____

_____

_____

_____

Monthly Calendar

Month: _____   **Year:** _____

Goals:

Notes:

_____
_____
_____
_____
_____
_____

Monthly Calendar

Month: _____   **Year:** _____

Goals:

Notes:

_____

_____

_____

_____

_____

_____

Monthly Calendar

Month: _____   Year: _____

Goals:

Notes:

_____

_____

_____

_____

_____

_____

Monthly Calendar

Month: _____ Year: _____

Goals:

Notes:

_____

_____

_____

_____

_____

_____

Monthly Calendar

Month: _____ Year: _____

Goals:

Notes:

_____

_____

_____

_____

_____

_____

Monthly Calendar

Month: _____   Year: _____

Goals:

Notes:

_____
_____
_____
_____
_____
_____

Monthly Calendar

Month: _____   Year: _____

Goals:

Notes:

_____

_____

_____

_____

_____

_____

Monthly Calendar

Month: _____   **Year:** _____

Goals:

Notes:

_____

_____

_____

_____

_____

_____

SLAY THE DAY

It is not always easy to step out of your comfort zone; after all, you've grown so accustomed to it. But, TODAY... You will slay every mindset that is holding you back, all of your fears, and get comfortable being uncomfortable. Being You... and not apologizing for it!

Road Map to Success

There is only one you, so take a stroll with me and together become stronger, enabled, empowered, equipped, and ready to receive everything God has in store for you. Why? Because You Matter and You're Worth It!

1
Emotional - It's okay, emotions are feelings and they are fleeting. How are you feeling today? Get to know what triggers your emotions and set some boundaries.

Learn to let go of your inhibitions without apology. Let go of toxic people, cry if you must, but set new goals for success.

2
In all things practice restraint. Create a realistic budget, reorganize a closet, implement a daily self-care routine, drink more water!

It is perfectly fine and a must, to love yourself! Self-care is essential. Taking time for your personal sanity is not selfish.

3
Lets get physical! Yup, being up and active helps not only our curves but also enhances are mood ~ total win-win!! But, being physical is not just about exercise, it's also about touch and self-care.

Do something nice for you today, take a walk, a much needed nap, soak in the tub, or try a new hairstyle.

4
Mind * Body * and Soul. Read and repeat inspirational affirmations, focus on the present, take a road trip, hug someone, take a friend to lunch, have a couples night, pray, volunteer, partake in random acts of kindness!

Be kind to yourself :)

Section 1

Emotional

Self-Care Checklist

☐ Writing in a journal

☐ Creating art

☐ Playing music

☐ Starting a gratitude journal

☐ Add rest time to your schedule

☐ Practice meditation & awareness

☐ Learn to say "No" and serve yourself first

☐ Protect your energy from others

☐ Ask for help when you feel overwhelmed

☐ Experience your emotions without judgement

- [ ] Get to know your emotional triggers
- [ ] Do something you love each day
- [ ] Set boundaries
- [ ] Stop apologizing for everything
- [ ] Accept compliments
- [ ] Write a "love letter" to yourself
- [ ] Say one thing you love about your body
- [ ] forgive yourself for small mistakes
- [ ] Have a good long cry
- [ ] Start a list of great things people say about you
- [ ] Re-visit happy times by reading old emails or letters
- [ ] Take 15 minutes to write down anything that's bothering you, then throw the paper away
- [ ] Read some feel good quotes or poetry
- [ ] Recite self-love affirmations
- [ ] Fill in the blank "I Love myself because.."
- [ ] Try adult coloring

How Balanced Are You?

Try out the balance wheel and find out!
Shade in the level that each area takes up in your life.

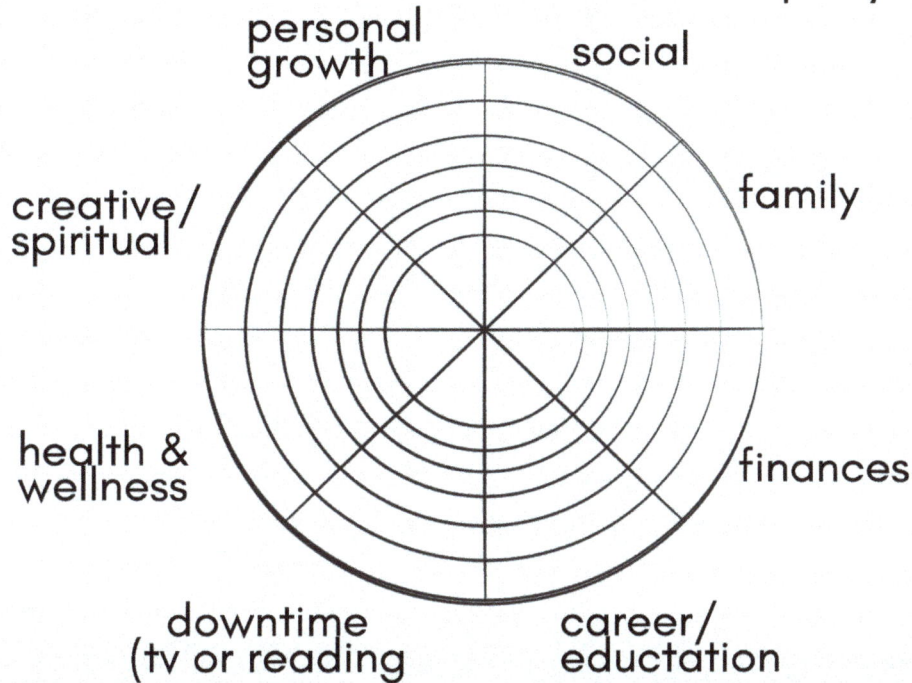

personal growth

social

creative/ spiritual

family

health & wellness

finances

downtime (tv or reading

career/ eductation

Create a Plan to Find More Balance

Personal Growth: _____

Social: _____

Family: _____

Finances: _____

Career/Education: _____

Downtime: _____

Health/Wellness: _____

Creative/Spiritual: _____

Daily Check In

Date:

| Jan | Feb | Mar | Apr | May | Jun | Jul | Aug | Sep | Oct | Nov | Dec |

1 2 3 4 5 6 7 8 9 10 11 12 13 14 15 16 17 18 19 20 21 22 **23** 24 25 26 27 **28** 29 30 **31**

How's It Going Today?

5 hearts for super ranging to 1 heart for not so well

Health    **Family**

Work    **Friends**

Energy    **Overall**

How I reacted at my lowest point of the day:

What I learned about myself today:

How I reacted at my highest point of the day:

Daily Check In

Date:

Jan	Feb	Mar	Apr	May	Jun	Jul	Aug	Sep	Oct	Nov	Dec

1 2 3 4 5 6 7 8 9 10 11 12 13 14 15 16 17 18 19 20 21 22 23 24 25 26 27 28 29 30 31

How's It Going Today?

5 hearts for super ranging to 1 heart for not so well

 ♡ ♡ ♡ ♡ ♡    ♡ ♡ ♡ ♡ ♡

 ♡ ♡ ♡ ♡ ♡    ♡ ♡ ♡ ♡ ♡

 ♡ ♡ ♡ ♡ ♡    ♡ ♡ ♡ ♡ ♡

How I reacted at my lowest point of the day:

What I learned about myself today:

How I reacted at my highest point of the day:

Daily Check In

Date:

| Jan | Feb | Mar | Apr | May | Jun | Jul | Aug | Sep | Oct | Nov | Dec |

1 2 3 4 5 6 7 8 9 10 11 12 13 14 15 16 17 18 19 20 21 22 **23** 24 25 26 27 **28** 29 30 **31**

How's It Going Today?

5 hearts for super ranging to 1 heart for not so well

Health ♡ ♡ ♡ ♡ ♡   **Family** ♡ ♡ ♡ ♡ ♡

Work ♡ ♡ ♡ ♡ ♡   **Friends** ♡ ♡ ♡ ♡ ♡

Energy ♡ ♡ ♡ ♡ ♡   **Overall** ♡ ♡ ♡ ♡ ♡

How I reacted at my
lowest point of the day:

What I learned about
myself today:

How I reacted at my
highest point of the day:

Daily Check In

Date:

| Jan | Feb | Mar | Apr | May | Jun | Jul | Aug | Sep | Oct | Nov | Dec |

1 2 3 4 5 6 7 8 9 10 11 12 13 14 15 16 17 18 19 20 21 22 23 24 25 26 27 28 29 30 31

How's It Going Today?

5 hearts for super ranging to 1 heart for not so well

Health    **Family**

Work    **Friends**

Energy    **Overall**

How I reacted at my lowest point of the day:

What I learned about myself today:

How I reacted at my highest point of the day:

Daily Check In

Date:

| Jan | Feb | Mar | Apr | May | Jun | Jul | Aug | Sep | Oct | Nov | Dec |

1 2 3 4 5 6 7 8 9 10 11 12 13 14 15 16 17 18 19 20 21 22 **23** 24 25 26 27 28 29 30 **31**

How's It Going Today?

5 hearts for super ranging to 1 heart for not so well

Health ♡♡♡♡♡   **Family** ♡♡♡♡♡

Work ♡♡♡♡♡   **Friends** ♡♡♡♡♡

Energy ♡♡♡♡♡   **Overall** ♡♡♡♡♡

How I reacted at my
lowest point of the day:

What I learned about
myself today:

How I reacted at my
highest point of the day:

Daily Check In

Jan	Feb	Mar	Apr	May	Jun	Jul	Aug	Sep	Oct	Nov	Dec

1 2 3 4 5 6 7 8 9 10 11 12 13 14 15 16 17 18 19 20 21 22 23 24 25 26 27 28 29 30 31

How's It Going Today?

5 hearts for super ranging to 1 heart for not so well

 Health ♡ ♡ ♡ ♡ ♡    Family ♡ ♡ ♡ ♡ ♡

 Work ♡ ♡ ♡ ♡ ♡    Friends ♡ ♡ ♡ ♡ ♡

 Energy ♡ ♡ ♡ ♡ ♡    Overall ♡ ♡ ♡ ♡ ♡

How I reacted at my
lowest point of the day:

What I learned about
myself today:

How I reacted at my
highest point of the day:

Daily Check In

Date:

| Jan | Feb | Mar | Apr | May | Jun | Jul | Aug | Sep | Oct | Nov | Dec |

1 2 3 4 5 6 7 8 9 10 11 12 13 14 15 16 17 18 19 20 21 22 **23** 24 25 26 27 **28** 29 30 **31**

How's It Going Today?

5 hearts for super ranging to 1 heart for not so well

Health    **Family**

Work    **Friends**

Energy    **Overall**

How I reacted at my
lowest point of the day:

What I learned about
myself today:

How I reacted at my
highest point of the day:

Daily Check In

Date:

| Jan | Feb | Mar | Apr | May | Jun | Jul | Aug | Sep | Oct | Nov | Dec |

1 2 3 4 5 6 7 8 9 10 11 12 13 14 15 16 17 18 19 20 21 22 23 24 25 26 27 28 29 30 31

How's It Going Today?

5 hearts for super ranging to 1 heart for not so well

Health    **Family**

Work    **Friends**

Energy    **Overall**

How I reacted at my
lowest point of the day:

What I learned about
myself today:

How I reacted at my
highest point of the day:

Daily Check In

| Jan | Feb | Mar | Apr | May | Jun | Jul | Aug | Sep | Oct | Nov | Dec |

1 2 3 4 5 6 7 8 9 10 11 12 13 14 15 16 17 18 19 20 21 22 **23** 24 25 26 27 **28** 29 30 **31**

How's It Going Today?

5 hearts for super ranging to 1 heart for not so well

Health ♡ ♡ ♡ ♡ ♡   **Family** ♡ ♡ ♡ ♡ ♡

Work ♡ ♡ ♡ ♡ ♡   **Friends** ♡ ♡ ♡ ♡ ♡

Energy ♡ ♡ ♡ ♡ ♡   **Overall** ♡ ♡ ♡ ♡ ♡

How I reacted at my
lowest point of the day:

What I learned about
myself today:

How I reacted at my
highest point of the day:

Daily Check In

Date:

| Jan | Feb | Mar | Apr | May | Jun | Jul | Aug | Sep | Oct | Nov | Dec |

1   2   3   4   5   6   7   8   9   10   11   12   13   14   15   16   17   18   19   20   21   22   23   24   25   26   27   28   29   30   31

How's It Going Today?

5 hearts for super ranging to 1 heart for not so well

 Health ♡ ♡ ♡ ♡ ♡    Family ♡ ♡ ♡ ♡ ♡

 Work ♡ ♡ ♡ ♡ ♡    Friends ♡ ♡ ♡ ♡ ♡

 Energy ♡ ♡ ♡ ♡ ♡    Overall ♡ ♡ ♡ ♡ ♡

How I reacted at my lowest point of the day:

What I learned about myself today:

How I reacted at my highest point of the day:

Daily Check In

Date:

Jan	Feb	Mar	Apr	May	Jun	Jul	Aug	Sep	Oct	Nov	Dec

1 2 3 4 5 6 7 8 9 10 11 12 13 14 15 16 17 18 19 20 21 22 23 24 25 26 27 28 29 30 31

How's It Going Today?

5 hearts for super ranging to 1 heart for not so well

Health ♡ ♡ ♡ ♡ ♡   **Family** ♡ ♡ ♡ ♡ ♡

Work ♡ ♡ ♡ ♡ ♡   **Friends** ♡ ♡ ♡ ♡ ♡

Energy ♡ ♡ ♡ ♡ ♡   **Overall** ♡ ♡ ♡ ♡ ♡

How I reacted at my
lowest point of the day:

What I learned about
myself today:

How I reacted at my
highest point of the day:

Daily Check In

Date:

Jan	Feb	Mar	Apr	May	Jun	Jul	Aug	Sep	Oct	Nov	Dec

1 2 3 4 5 6 7 8 9 10 11 12 13 14 15 16 17 18 19 20 21 22 23 24 25 26 27 28 29 30 31

How's It Going Today?

5 hearts for super ranging to 1 heart for not so well

 ♡ ♡ ♡ ♡ ♡    ♡ ♡ ♡ ♡ ♡

 ♡ ♡ ♡ ♡ ♡    ♡ ♡ ♡ ♡ ♡

 ♡ ♡ ♡ ♡ ♡    ♡ ♡ ♡ ♡ ♡

How I reacted at my
lowest point of the day:

What I learned about
myself today:

How I reacted at my
highest point of the day:

Daily Check In

Date:

Jan	Feb	Mar	Apr	May	Jun	Jul	Aug	Sep	Oct	Nov	Dec

1 2 3 4 5 6 7 8 9 10 11 12 13 14 15 16 17 18 19 20 21 22 **23** 24 25 26 27 **28** 29 30 **31**

How's It Going Today?

5 hearts for super ranging to 1 heart for not so well

Health    **Family**

Work    **Friends**

Energy    **Overall**

How I reacted at my
lowest point of the day:

What I learned about
myself today:

How I reacted at my
highest point of the day:

Daily Check In

How's It Going Today?

5 hearts for super ranging to 1 heart for not so well

 **Health** ♡ ♡ ♡ ♡ ♡    **Family** ♡ ♡ ♡ ♡ ♡

 **Work** ♡ ♡ ♡ ♡ ♡    **Friends** ♡ ♡ ♡ ♡ ♡

 **Energy** ♡ ♡ ♡ ♡ ♡    **Overall** ♡ ♡ ♡ ♡ ♡

How I reacted at my
lowest point of the day:

What I learned about
myself today:

How I reacted at my
highest point of the day:

Daily Check In

How's It Going Today?

5 hearts for super ranging to 1 heart for not so well

Health ♡ ♡ ♡ ♡ ♡   **Family** ♡ ♡ ♡ ♡ ♡

Work ♡ ♡ ♡ ♡ ♡   **Friends** ♡ ♡ ♡ ♡ ♡

Energy ♡ ♡ ♡ ♡ ♡   **Overall** ♡ ♡ ♡ ♡ ♡

How I reacted at my lowest point of the day:

What I learned about myself today:

How I reacted at my highest point of the day:

Journal Time

WRITE ABOUT ONE THING THAT MAKES YOU HAPPY

Today, You are the only priority. You cannot pour from an empty vessel.

_____

_____

_____

_____

_____

_____

_____

_____

_____

_____

_____

_____

Section 2

Practical

Self-Care Checklist

- [ ] Create a budget

- [ ] Take a NEW course

- [ ] Organize a closet or space

- [ ] Make a healthy lunch the night before

- [ ] Set a schedule and stick to it!

- [ ] Implement your daily self-care routine

- [ ] Put all of your outfits together for the week

- [ ] Sunday night fill up your gas tank

- [ ] Learn a NEW helpful skill

- [ ] Organize your desk at home or work

Shopping List

BUDGET

Shopping List

BUDGET

Saving PLANNER

WEEK	AMOUNT	BALANCE	✔
01			
02			
03			
04			
05			
06			
07			
08			
09			
10			
11			
12			
13			
14			
15			
16			
17			
18			
19			
20			

WEEK	AMOUNT	BALANCE	✔
01			
02			
03			
04			
05			
06			
07			
08			
09			
10			
11			
12			
13			
14			
15			
16			
17			
18			
19			
20			

Saving PLANNER

WEEK	AMOUNT	BALANCE	✔	WEEK	AMOUNT	BALANCE	✔
01				01			
02				02			
03				03			
04				04			
05				05			
06				06			
07				07			
08				08			
09				09			
10				10			
11				11			
12				12			
13				13			
14				14			
15				15			
16				16			
17				17			
18				18			
19				19			
20				20			

Debt Payment TRACKER

TYPE:

MIN.PAYMENT:

TOTAL PAYMENT:

PAID	BALANCE
Month 1	
Month 2	
Month 3	
Month 4	
Month 5	
Month 6	
Month 7	
Month 8	
Month 9	
Month 10	
Month 11	
Month 12	

PAID	BALANCE
Month 1	
Month 2	
Month 3	
Month 4	
Month 5	
Month 6	
Month 7	
Month 8	
Month 9	
Month 10	
Month 11	
Month 12	

Debt Payment TRACKER

TYPE:

MIN.PAYMENT:

TOTAL PAYMENT:

PAID	BALANCE		PAID	BALANCE
Month 1			Month 1	
Month 2			Month 2	
Month 3			Month 3	
Month 4			Month 4	
Month 5			Month 5	
Month 6			Month 6	
Month 7			Month 7	
Month 8			Month 8	
Month 9			Month 9	
Month 10			Month 10	
Month 11			Month 11	
Month 12			Month 12	

Monthly Bill TRACKER

MONTH												AMOUNT	BILL
J	F	M	A	M	J	J	A	S	O	N	D		

Never get so busy making a living that you forget to make a life!
DOLLY PARTON

DATE:

Journal Time

_____

_____

_____

_____

_____

_____

_____

_____

_____

_____

_____

Section 3

Physical
Self-Care Checklist

☐ Start a healthy meal plan

☐ Do it yourself mani/pedi

☐ Take a swim

☐ Jump on a trampoline

☐ Try a new hairstyle

☐ Floss everyday

☐ Start a skin care routine

☐ Stop biting your nails

☐ Moisturize

☐ Paint your nails

☐ Take a 20 min nap

- [ ] Dance to your favorite song
- [ ] Try yoga
- [ ] Drink more water
- [ ] Get a massage
- [ ] Got to bed early
- [ ] Try hiking or camping
- [ ] Join a walking group
- [ ] Take a gym class
- [ ] Take a long shower
- [ ] Take a bubble bath
- [ ] Try acupuncture
- [ ] Get a physical at the doctors
- [ ] Stay up to date on all other Dr's appts
- [ ] Observe nature outside
- [ ] Schedule a spa day

Fitness Tracker

Goal Weight: _____

CALORIES INTAKE	EXERCISE		

MONDAY

CALORIES INTAKE

Breakfast _____
Lunch _____
Dinner _____
Snacks _____ Beverages _____
TOTAL CALORIES INTAKE:

EXERCISE

TYPE	TIME	CAL BURNED

TOTAL CALORIES BURNED:

TUESDAY

CALORIES INTAKE

Breakfast _____
Lunch _____
Dinner _____
Snacks _____ Beverages _____
TOTAL CALORIES INTAKE:

EXERCISE

TYPE	TIME	CAL BURNED

TOTAL CALORIES BURNED:

WEDNESDAY

CALORIES INTAKE

Breakfast _____
Lunch _____
Dinner _____
Snacks _____ Beverages _____
TOTAL CALORIES INTAKE:

EXERCISE

TYPE	TIME	CAL BURNED

TOTAL CALORIES BURNED:

THURSDAY

CALORIES INTAKE

Breakfast _____
Lunch _____
Dinner _____
Snacks _____ Beverages _____
TOTAL CALORIES INTAKE:

EXERCISE

TYPE	TIME	CAL BURNED

TOTAL CALORIES BURNED:

FRIDAY

CALORIES INTAKE

Breakfast _____
Lunch _____
Dinner _____
Snacks _____ Beverages _____
TOTAL CALORIES INTAKE:

EXERCISE

TYPE	TIME	CAL BURNED

TOTAL CALORIES BURNED:

SATURDAY

CALORIES INTAKE

Breakfast _____
Lunch _____
Dinner _____
Snacks _____ Beverages _____
TOTAL CALORIES INTAKE:

EXERCISE

TYPE	TIME	CAL BURNED

TOTAL CALORIES BURNED:

SUNDAY

CALORIES INTAKE

Breakfast _____
Lunch _____
Dinner _____
Snacks _____ Beverages _____
TOTAL CALORIES INTAKE:

EXERCISE

TYPE	TIME	CAL BURNED

TOTAL CALORIES BURNED:

MY WORKOUT CHALLENGE

TODAY I DID...

- ☐ 20 SQUATS

- ☐ 10 PUSH UPS

- ☐ 20 LUNGES

- ☐ 10 DUMBELL LIFTS

- ☐ 15-SECOND PLANK

- ☐ 30 JUMPING JACKS

YOU CAN NEVER EXPECT TO SUCCEED IF YOU ONLY PUT IN WORK ON THE DAYS YOU FEEL LIKE IT.

GOAL
Getter

GOAL FOR THE DAY

START:

_____

FINISH:

_____

IDEAS

....
....
....
....
....
....
....
....
....
....
....

THINGS NEEDED:

REFERENCES:

ACTION STEPS

1. _____ ◯
2. _____ ◯
3. _____ ◯
4. _____ ◯
5. _____ ◯
6. _____ ◯
7. _____ ◯
8. _____ ◯

NOTES:

I can & I will

YOU CAN NEVER
EXPECT TO SUCCEED IF
YOU ONLY PUT IN WORK
ON THE DAYS YOU FEEL
LIKE IT.

GOAL Getter

GOAL FOR THE DAY

START:

_____

FINISH:

_____

IDEAS

....
....
....
....
....
....
....
....
....
....
....
....

THINGS NEEDED:

REFERENCES:

ACTION STEPS

1. _____ ◯
2. _____ ◯
3. _____ ◯
4. _____ ◯
5. _____ ◯
6. _____ ◯
7. _____ ◯
8. _____ ◯

NOTES:

I can & I will

YOU CAN NEVER EXPECT TO SUCCEED IF YOU ONLY PUT IN WORK ON THE DAYS YOU FEEL LIKE IT.

GOAL Getter

GOAL FOR THE DAY

START:

_____

FINISH:

_____

IDEAS

....
....
....
....
....
....
....
....
....
....

THINGS NEEDED:

REFERENCES:

ACTION STEPS

1. _____ ◯
2. _____ ◯
3. _____ ◯
4. _____ ◯
5. _____ ◯
6. _____ ◯
7. _____ ◯
8. _____ ◯

NOTES:

I can & I will

DATE:

Journal Time

WHAT DOES SELF-CARE MEAN TO YOU? WHAT DOES IT LOOK AND FEEL LIKE? WRITE ABOUT THAT

You are enough, You are fearless, You are strong, You are gorgeous!

_____

_____

_____

_____

_____

_____

_____

_____

_____

_____

_____

_____

Section 4

Mind, Body, & Soul

Self-Care Checklist

- [ ] Focusing on the present
- [ ] Write a to do list to clear your mind
- [ ] Don't rush yourself
- [ ] Take one thing at a time
- [ ] Mediatation
- [ ] Take a mental break to be alone for 15 mins
- [ ] Detach from all social media
- [ ] Say no to gossip
- [ ] Listen to a good TED talk or Podcast
- [ ] Listen to a motivational video on Youtube

- [ ] Go with a friend to run errands
- [ ] Call a friend or family member to say hi
- [ ] Cuddle someone or give a hug!
- [ ] Have a picnic with family of friends
- [ ] Get to know your neighbors
- [ ] Schedule a date night
- [ ] Schedule a girls night out
- [ ] Go for a quick trip out of town with friends
- [ ] Road trip with siblings
- [ ] Take a friend to lunch
- [ ] Visit relatives
- [ ] Have a family dinner
- [ ] Say YES to an RSVP for an event
- [ ] Plan a BBQ
- [ ] Join a class, group, or team
- [ ] Join a community event

- [ ] Make time for meditation daily
- [ ] Attend a church or spiritual community service
- [ ] Donate to a charity
- [ ] Pray
- [ ] Practice relaxation techniques
- [ ] Memorize passages from the bible or religious text
- [ ] Take a social media break
- [ ] Practice empathy
- [ ] Try random acts of kindness
- [ ] Volunteer
- [ ] Spend time in nature
- [ ] Create an inspiring vision board
- [ ] Intentionally observe nature
- [ ] Be still and quiet for 10 mins
- [ ] Read inspirational quotes or literature
- [ ] Practice forgiveness

- [ ] Bake something for fun
- [ ] Book a night in a fancy hotel
- [ ] Buy some flowers that you love
- [ ] Get a treat from the grocery store
- [ ] Eat your favorite comfort foods
- [ ] Go see a movie by yourself
- [ ] Go wine tasting
- [ ] moisturize your feet and wear socks
- [ ] Order in dinner
- [ ] Have someone clean your house
- [ ] Splurge on skincare
- [ ] Make a hair appointment
- [ ] Make a reservation at your favorite restaurant
- [ ] Get a facial
- [ ] Visit a waxing salon
- [ ] Buy a plushy robe

30 Days of Affirmations

Fill Your Month Affirming Your Value

Each square represents one day of the month. Mark the box when you have fulfilled the day. Let's try to leave no box unchecked!

I am worthy	My past DOES NOT Dictate My future	I Am Allowed to Say NO	I Am Healthy	Kindness is free
This is Tough, but so am I	There is Power within me	The money I spend is always replaced with more	Never give up on you	I am secure
I deserve to be Loved	I Ask, I Believe, I Receive	Happiness is a choice, I choose it daily	I am grateful	Fear of failure does not control me
It's OKAY to Not Know everything	I accept and love myself for who I AM	I listen to the needs of my body with love	My life is rich with opportunities	I am Courageous
I Am happy	I Am beautiful	Prosperity flows to and from me	I choose Love, Not Fear	I Am letting go of what no longer serves me
I see beauty in all things	I am Enough	I will never give up on my goals & dreams	Today Will Be Another Successful Day	I am Blessed

The best care is Self Care

Thought Reframing

My thought:

Is this thought true & do I have evidence?

On a scale of 1 to 10, how big is this issue to me?

♡ ♡ ♡ ♡ ♡ ♡ ♡ ♡ ♡ ♡

Is there something actionable I can do?

◯ YES　　　◯ NO

If yes, what will I do? If no, what are ways
I can move past the thought?

Reframing the thought:

Thought Reframing

My thought:

On a scale of 1 to 10, how big is this issue to me?

♡ ♡ ♡ ♡ ♡ ♡ ♡ ♡ ♡ ♡

Is there something actionable I can do?

○ YES   ○ NO

If yes, what will I do? If no, what are ways
I can move past the thought?

Reframing the thought:

Thought Reframing

My thought:

Is this thought true & do I have evidence?

On a scale of 1 to 10, how big is this issue to me?

♡ ♡ ♡ ♡ ♡ ♡ ♡ ♡ ♡ ♡

Is there something actionable I can do?

◯ YES   ◯ NO

If yes, what will I do? If no, what are ways
I can move past the thought?

Reframing the thought:

What is motivating you to achieve your goals and what habits are you forming to push you were you want to be?

MOTIVATION GETS YOU STARTED, HABIT KEEPS YOU GOING.

- Jim Ryan

Habit Tracker

Log Your Daily Habits for a Month

Fill in the habit you want to track and your goal for changing or maintaining the habit.

Habit: _____

Goal: _____

S	M	T	W	T	F	S
☐	☐	☐	☐	☐	☐	☐
☐	☐	☐	☐	☐	☐	☐
☐	☐	☐	☐	☐	☐	☐
☐	☐	☐	☐	☐	☐	☐
☐	☐	☐	☐	☐	☐	☐

Habit: _____

Goal: _____

S	M	T	W	T	F	S
☐	☐	☐	☐	☐	☐	☐
☐	☐	☐	☐	☐	☐	☐
☐	☐	☐	☐	☐	☐	☐
☐	☐	☐	☐	☐	☐	☐
☐	☐	☐	☐	☐	☐	☐

Habit: _____

Goal: _____

S	M	T	W	T	F	S
☐	☐	☐	☐	☐	☐	☐
☐	☐	☐	☐	☐	☐	☐
☐	☐	☐	☐	☐	☐	☐
☐	☐	☐	☐	☐	☐	☐
☐	☐	☐	☐	☐	☐	☐

Habit: _____

Goal: _____

S	M	T	W	T	F	S
☐	☐	☐	☐	☐	☐	☐
☐	☐	☐	☐	☐	☐	☐
☐	☐	☐	☐	☐	☐	☐
☐	☐	☐	☐	☐	☐	☐
☐	☐	☐	☐	☐	☐	☐

Habit Tracker

Log Your Daily Habits for a Month

Fill in the habit you want to track and your goal for changing or maintaining the habit.

Habit: _____

S	M	T	W	T	F	S
☐	☐	☐	☐	☐	☐	☐
☐	☐	☐	☐	☐	☐	☐
☐	☐	☐	☐	☐	☐	☐
☐	☐	☐	☐	☐	☐	☐
☐	☐	☐	☐	☐	☐	☐

Goal: _____

Habit: _____

S	M	T	W	T	F	S
☐	☐	☐	☐	☐	☐	☐
☐	☐	☐	☐	☐	☐	☐
☐	☐	☐	☐	☐	☐	☐
☐	☐	☐	☐	☐	☐	☐
☐	☐	☐	☐	☐	☐	☐

Goal: _____

Habit: _____

S	M	T	W	T	F	S
☐	☐	☐	☐	☐	☐	☐
☐	☐	☐	☐	☐	☐	☐
☐	☐	☐	☐	☐	☐	☐
☐	☐	☐	☐	☐	☐	☐
☐	☐	☐	☐	☐	☐	☐

Goal: _____

Habit: _____

S	M	T	W	T	F	S
☐	☐	☐	☐	☐	☐	☐
☐	☐	☐	☐	☐	☐	☐
☐	☐	☐	☐	☐	☐	☐
☐	☐	☐	☐	☐	☐	☐
☐	☐	☐	☐	☐	☐	☐

Goal: _____

Habit Tracker

Log Your Daily Habits for a Month

Fill in the habit you want to track and your goal for changing or maintaining the habit.

Habit: _____

Goal: _____

S M T W T F S
☐ ☐ ☐ ☐ ☐ ☐ ☐
☐ ☐ ☐ ☐ ☐ ☐ ☐
☐ ☐ ☐ ☐ ☐ ☐ ☐
☐ ☐ ☐ ☐ ☐ ☐ ☐
☐ ☐ ☐ ☐ ☐ ☐ ☐

Habit: _____

Goal: _____

S M T W T F S
☐ ☐ ☐ ☐ ☐ ☐ ☐
☐ ☐ ☐ ☐ ☐ ☐ ☐
☐ ☐ ☐ ☐ ☐ ☐ ☐
☐ ☐ ☐ ☐ ☐ ☐ ☐
☐ ☐ ☐ ☐ ☐ ☐ ☐

Habit: _____

Goal: _____

S M T W T F S
☐ ☐ ☐ ☐ ☐ ☐ ☐
☐ ☐ ☐ ☐ ☐ ☐ ☐
☐ ☐ ☐ ☐ ☐ ☐ ☐
☐ ☐ ☐ ☐ ☐ ☐ ☐
☐ ☐ ☐ ☐ ☐ ☐ ☐

Habit: _____

Goal: _____

S M T W T F S
☐ ☐ ☐ ☐ ☐ ☐ ☐
☐ ☐ ☐ ☐ ☐ ☐ ☐
☐ ☐ ☐ ☐ ☐ ☐ ☐
☐ ☐ ☐ ☐ ☐ ☐ ☐
☐ ☐ ☐ ☐ ☐ ☐ ☐

Journal Time

BE HONEST AND ACCOUNTABLE TO YOURSELF AND WRITE
ABOUT WHATEVER FREES YOU, LET GO OF PAST HURTS,
PRACTICE FORGIVENESS, AND LIVE FREE!

Focus on today, tomorrow has its own concerns.

_____

_____

_____

_____

_____

_____

_____

_____

_____

_____

_____

_____

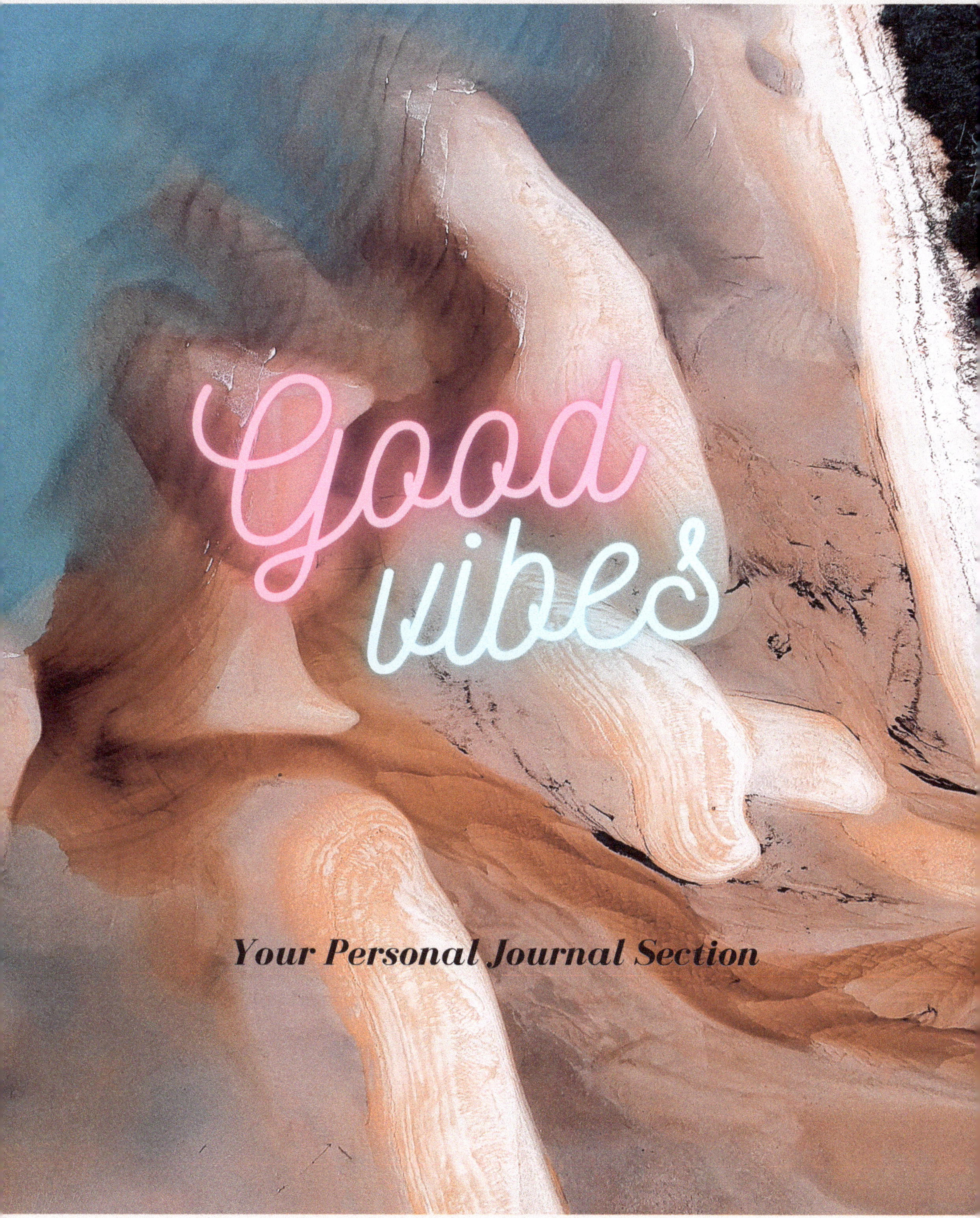

Your Personal Journal Section

DATE:

Journal Time

_____

_____

_____

_____

_____

_____

_____

_____

_____

_____

_____

_____

THANK
You

I hope you found this guide to self-care helpful in ensuring you take time out to care for yourself. I'd love to hear about it! Come, tell me about how you were most helped via the contact details below:

Toyia Caise
XOXO

IG: @BYTOYIACAISE
WWW.TOYIACAISE.COM
E: INFO@TOYIACAISE.COM

www.ingramcontent.com/pod-product-compliance
Lightning Source LLC
Chambersburg PA
CBHW051556030426

42334CB00034B/3452